ghosts.

Jessa Pinto

Presentation by *BookLeaf Publishing*

Web: www.bookleafpub.com

E-mail: info@bookleafpub.com

ISBN : 9789357699617

First edition 2022

somewhere.

as i sit by the river
staring at the skyline
i can't help but think of you.
you're so close
but so far away.
we never met
but i know you're real.
i know
you're out there.

aggrieved.

i handed you my heart
but you dropped it over and over
again.
glass shattered on the floor
torn pages of words

i never had the chance to say.

acquiesce.

i had no choice
but to set you free
as much as i wished
for you to stay here with me.

fragments.

another ghost in the graveyard
another dead butterfly in the jar
another skeleton in my closet
another monster under my bed
another memory tucked away in the attic
collecting dust.

apathy.

no more calls
he doesn't text
the jagged edge of the silence
tears your heart into pieces
how painful it is

someone regrets even knowing you.

calling.

if i called you
i'd say
"Meet me by the river.
I'm on the Hudson;

but only if you want to."

faded.

in my dreams
and daydreams
you call me
you text me and
tell me you miss me.
but this regret
is one-sided
and i remain
broken.

imprinted.

maybe the timing wasn't right.
maybe we weren't ready for each other.
or
maybe we were never right for each other in the
first place.

but i could never forget you.

smoke.

you were
the hands i never got to hold
the lips i never got to kiss
the skin i never got to touch
the embrace i never got to feel
the one i never got to love
we were
the story that was never meant to be told.

unspoken.

i never told you
but i hope you knew
how much i love you.

waiting.

i sat by the river today
and thought of you again.
the skyline so close i could touch it.
you're over there
but you don't know
that i'm here.

hopeless.

knowing you're out there
but not knowing you
leaves my heart a little broken.

stranger.

your soul is out there somewhere
living
breathing
laughing
crying
resting
maybe someday
i will hear it's echo in the breeze
and find you by the river
waiting for me.

gone.

the way you left
left me shattered.

contrition.

if i could
i would take back
all the words
that i wasted on you.

connected.

i sit here and wonder
if we are feeling the same breeze
through our hair.
feeling the same rain
on our skin.
hearing the same rush
of the water.

string.

maybe it's just the timing.
maybe someday
we'll get a second chance.
maybe someday
he'll come back to me.

torn.

but it was just as i had feared.
he was saying goodbye

for now.

candid.

i'm still hanging onto that hope that he'll come
back
though, i don't think he ever will.

affliction.

some goodbyes have the power to kill.
shatter hearts
rip souls apart
leave us lying on the floor
broken.

adieu.

you are a voice from my past
that i will never hear again.